THE LORD'S PRAYER

CAN YOU PRAY THE LORD'S PRAYER?

Dr. A. C. Johnson

THE LORD'S PRAYER

CAN YOU PRAY
THE LORD'S PRAYER?

DR. A. C. JOHNSON

PUBLISHED BY:
BRENTWOOD CHRISTIAN PRESS
4000 BEALLWOOD AVENUE
COLUMBUS, GEORGIA 31904

Dedication

To Him who taught us to pray

Acknowledgements

Grateful acknowledgements:--

1] Moody Press for permission to use illustrations. Chicago.

2] Rev. Douglas Friederichsen for use of the illustrations from the five great illustrated study books [1. God's Relief For Burdens. 2. God's Will Made Clear. 3. God's Way Made Easy. 4. God's Truth Made Simple. 5. God's Word Made Plain] by the missionary Paula Kay Friederichsen. Publishers, Moody press.

3] Publishers of the Word of God. The Bible quotations used are from KJV and NLT.

4] Leslie Samuel, Rajkumar Johnson and Satyabama Johnson for proof-reading.

Contents

Chapter 1

PRAYER

What is prayer?

Prayer is the craving of an empty heart for it's emptiness to be filled. The craving is for love, safety, security and comfort etc. It is the need of every human heart.

The law of nature on earth is to 'abhor any vacuum.' Something has to fill in that void. This is very applicable to our emotions. We all turn to either our Creator God, or, to what we make into a God, whether it be a material object, or a concept, or to the 'self', making the 'self' into a deity.

But when trials and storms of life beat upon us, only those who put their trust in God are able to cope with bad situations. Others are driven into depressions, or psychotic behaviors.

The Father
(THE KINGDOM)

THE SON
(THE GLORY)

FOR EVER AND EVER

MATH 6 : 9 - 13 : LUKE 11 : 2 - 4

THE HOLY SPIRIT
(THE POWER)

If upon the true God you do not pin your hope,
With life's many hardships you cannot cope.

Who needs prayer?

You and I do. We all have needs.

For, if we do not pray,
We will become a prey.

There are Four Different stages of prayer.

1]. "Give For Me" Stage of Prayers: - Many start their prayer by making a long list of things they would like to have. They may even prioritize the list. This is comparable to sitting in front of the T.V. Shopping channel and phoning for the 'tempting things' whether we really need them or not. Some of these prayers are answered. It does not mean that we are OK with God. God gives mercy to the just and to the unjust, making His sunlight and rain available to all, both to the good and the bad. People ask for health, life, wealth, cars, homes, beautiful rich wife, obedient daughters in law and children. Thieves ask for a good harvest and offer a share to 'god'. Armies pray for their enemies to be annihilated and safety for themselves. The basis of such asking is that 'I deserve it', much like the Prodigal Son asked for his share of the father's property, even when the father was alive, and this son deserved nothing. Answer to such prayers is possible even when we have no real connection to heaven. Our prayers will change when we really make a connection with God.

2]. "For-Give Me" Stage of Prayer---This is our very first prayer as we make our connection with God. All we desire in this prayer is to connect with God, and not with a desire for 'things' God can give us. Our desperate need is to come to this stage before we can proceed in our lives. It is during this prayer, that the pardon and salvation of the Lord is given to any one coming with this prayer. THE GUILT AND BURDEN OF SIN ARE REMOVED FROM THE ONE WHO PRAYS THIS PRAYER.

The Prodigal Son, having squandered all the wealth he got from the father ended up in the pig pen longing for the pig slop to assuage his hunger [and starvation to death]. So he finally did the right thing. He came to the father not expecting to be received back as a son, but as a lowly servant. And he said the right thing, by changing the order of his need to "FOR-GIVE me", and no more of "Give for ME". That prayer got him back into the father's family, as it will, you and me. This prayer gets us started in our lives, into an eternal relationship with God.

3]. The Stage "For,-getting ONE'S SELF" to learn to walk and to talk with God the Creator.

Like a new born takes much time and many tumbles before learning to walk, we have many ups and downs in life. Like as a child whines and cries, throwing tantrums before being able to say clearly it's needs, we ask for many harmful things. God has given an example of how an answer to a bad prayer can result in long lasting harm. An extension of life for king Hezekiah when God wanted him to prepare for the home call, resulted in a foolish display of the temple wealth by Hezekiah to the enemies, who robbed the wealth. What was even worse was that he sired a monster who mislead the entire nation into sin, wickedness and defiance to God

During this stage of prayer, we gradually learn to appreciate the will of God, and to submit to the perfect will of God. We will learn how to offer ourselves as "living sacrifices"-voluntarily, in total consecration. We also learn to willingly stay on the altar, and not "wriggle off the altar", or, alter our willingness when any wind blows to bring any chill upon our 'selves'.

4]. The ultimate Stage of prayer is "FORGETTING SELF" and to Intercede for Other's needs only, like Jesus did. The only desire is to do the will of God our Father in Heaven. Every Christian needs to grow to this prayer level.

Why should we pray?
People from all countries for centuries as far as we can trace back have known that prayer works. Skeptics have also found that prayer does work. Clinical studies done in major medical centers have shown that healing does occur more often and quicker for people that have been prayed over. The faith factor operates better with people who have faith in God. The prayer of trust enhances the immune system of the patients, and unexplainable healing occurs often.

Chapter 2

ACQUIRING KINSHIP WITH GOD

Where lays the 'Power of Prayer'?

Jesus who lived 2000 years ago showed the perfect way to live by living it Himself. He loved the unlovable, cared about them, moved and mingled with sinners, and yet remained pure. He cared more for others than for Himself. He prayed in the morning and at night, and in between. In fact, He was in constant touch with God. He was the one who introduced the truth that God is our Father, and not a terrifying powerful God who cared only for the elite Jews. This was one of the reasons that infuriated the religious leaders to such an extent that they planned to kill Jesus. But even while dying on the Cross Jesus showed the power of love by praying, for God to forgive the torturers and murderers.

The first four books of the New Testament give us first-hand information about the life and miracles of Jesus.

Josephus, a First Century historian documented that Jesus was a holy person who performed many miracles. These documents are available to this day.

Jesus trained a group of illiterate, simple people, and gave them power to do miraculous things. They were curious to know how Jesus, a simple carpenter could do such mighty things. Jesus revealed to them the source of His power as well as the purpose for His presence on earth:

[1]. That He was God who came down as a human to fulfill the many prophesies in the Old Testament of the Bible. The reason was to offer Himself as a blameless, holy human sacrifice to pay for humanity's sins and to bring pardon and eternal reconciliation with God the Father, the Creator.

2 Cor. 5:18-19 (NLT) All this newness of life is from God, who brought us back to Himself through what Christ did. And God has given us the task of reconciling people to Him. [19] For God was in Christ, reconciling the world to Himself, no longer counting people's sins against them. This is the wonderful message He has given us to tell others.

[2]. To show us human beings how to live holy, loving, caring lives pleasing to God, and to fulfill the purpose for which God created our lives on earth. He offered to become our role model on earth. To do this, He willingly laid aside His godliness and became an ordinary human being rather than even be as a king or a man of reputation. He chose to come to earth as a carpenter. He did not use His personal Godly powers to live a clean life or to perform great miracles. He used constant prayer to link Himself with God the Father, and drew upon God's power to live the way He did and to do the things He did.

Philip. 2:5-8 Your attitude should be the same that Christ Jesus had. [6] Though he was God, he did not demand and cling to his rights as God. [7] He made himself nothing; he took the humble position of a slave and appeared in human form. [8] And in human form he obediently humbled himself even further by dying a criminal's death on a cross.

We may wonder, how one could have the power to do miracles? Jesus healed the sick, caused the blind to see, caused the deaf to hear, fed more than 5000 men with nothing but 5 loaves of bread and few fishes. He even raised people from the dead, such as Lazarus 4 days after he was buried and rotting away. These incidents are well documented by Matthew an ex-tax collector, Mark, Luke a physician, and John one of His disciples in the four gospels of the New Testament. Jesus even gave power to the disciples to do miracles and heal the sick. What was the power working in Jesus? It was [and still is] PRAYER.

The disciples knew that Jesus prayed not only in the morning and night, but also at all times. Jesus told His disciples that He could do NOTHING by Himself, except through the FATHER.

> *John 5:19 Jesus replied, "I assure you, the Son can do nothing by himself. He does only what he sees the Father doing. Whatever the Father does, the Son also does.*

Jesus was in constant contact with God the Father, the Creator of all things, who has the power greater than high-voltage electricity. It is only when one is in unbroken touch [contact] with God, could one live like Jesus and perform miracles like Jesus did.

> *John 14:10 Believest thou not that I am in the Father, and the Father in me? the words that I speak unto you I speak not of myself: but the Father that dwelleth in me, he doeth the works*

> *John 11:41-45 So they rolled the stone aside. Then Jesus looked up to heaven and said, "<u>Father, thank you for hearing me. [42] You always hear me,</u> but I said it out loud for the sake of all these people standing here, so they will believe you sent me." [43] Then Jesus shouted, "Lazarus, come out!" [44] And Lazarus came out, bound in grave-clothes, his face wrapped in a head-cloth. Jesus told them, "Unwrap him and let him go!" [45] Many of the people who were with Mary believed in Jesus when they saw this happen.*

Jesus made it plain that when we repent and pray for God to forgive our sins, He does it on the basis of the sacrifice of Jesus on our behalf upon the Cross. As shown above, this prayer establishes reconciliation with God. Jesus said that He came down to earth to welcome all those who are willing to accept His Father's invitation for eternal life in God the Father's kingdom.

When the disciples wanted Jesus to teach them how to pray, He showed them what is prayer and what is not.

He taught them to pray, and us, how not to pray prayers that have no value.

He told us to cleanse our minds of anger, lust, divisions, retaliations, and grudges first. [Read Math cpt.5, 6, 7] before we can pray effectively

That prayer is not to be a 'show' to impress others. It is an intimate communication with the holy, mighty God who knows what is in our hearts, and not just what comes out of our mouths.

Commendable social services are not prayer. The work was done by Jesus, and there is nothing more for us to add to it, for the work is completed already.

A group of Christians with one accord in prayer have been promised a response from heaven. Non Christians try group collaboration to bend people's minds to theirs, but cannot influence heaven

Going to church regularly and being deeply involved in church activities does not replace prayer.

Churchianity and Christianity are not synonymous; they are not the same.

Repetitive chanting, bead rolling, is not prayer and does not influence God.

How often should we pray? David prayed at-least 'seven' times a day. God recommends prayer without ceasing. Our every inspiration should be to breathe in His love, and every natural expiration of our breath should become a prayer of thanksgiving, praise, worship, witnessing, or an intercession.

Prayer is not like rubbing the mythical Aladdin's lamp to get one's wishes fulfilled by a genie.

Fasting and prayer are for our good, and will not manipulate God.

Prayer for the permissive will of God brings upon us problems.

Praying in the Perfect Will of the Father God brings the Peace of God into our lives and others.

[Prayer of the Lord for His followers is different from the Lord's Prayer. Prayer of the Lord for His followers, is recorded in the 17th chapter of the gospel of John.]

So, Jesus gave us the "LORD'S PRAYER" to pray.

The Lord's Prayer is a short One, yet, it has three segments. It shows the inclusion of the Triune God and the role of the Trinity.

The first part deals with us submitting to the Father's role and rule, and becoming citizen in God's kingdom. It is an invitation from God to all.

The second part deals with us, to admit Jesus into our lives as our Lord, who will enable us to love, forgive others, and live like Jesus did. Jesus offers to become our daily Bread, as well as the Living and Life giving Water.

The third part shows us the power within our reach when we permit [obey] the Holy Spirit of God to be our constant guide, controller and advisor. The Holy Spirit endows us with God's power to sanctify us [to be Crucified with Jesus], and do mighty things [to let Christ to live in us and be glorified through us], to fulfill God's purpose victoriously through us.

Can you pray the Lord's Prayer?

Chapter 3

ACKNOWLEDGING
THE KINGSHIP OF GOD

The Lord's Prayer calls for: -

1. Acquiring KINSHIP with God.

2. Acknowledging the KINGSHIP of God.

3. Accepting the Responsibility of CITIZENSHIP

4. Accepting LORDSHIP of the Son of God.

5. Restoring the RELATIONSHIP with our neighbors, even people we don't like.

6. Submitting to the DISCIPLESHIP by the Holy Spirit.

7. Enlisting into God's WARSHIP to battle evil.

8. Learning to WORSHIP the Triune God.

The Lord's Prayer talks about the kingdom of God and offers an invitation for us to become citizens of His kingdom. We all are in an earthly kingdom, and are alien to God's kingdom. God's love for us is great and He is willing to receive us into His Kingdom. Every person who wants to become the citizen of another country needs to know and accept the conditions, rules, regulations, life-style of the country he/she wants to migrate to, to live in. Each person must go through a process called Immigration Naturalization Service ["I.N.S."]. There is a restriction of what can be carried into the country as personal belongings. This is checked by the customs inspection to keep out harmful things being smuggled or brought into the country, which will adversely affect the eco-system and the future good of the host country.

Jesus came to help us to go through the "I.N.S." – immigration, naturalization service, to become a citizen in God's eternal kingdom.

I – Invitation is from the Father.

N - Naturalization is done by the Son of God.

S - Sealed and secured by the Holy Spirit.

Information about God's Kingdom

In this kingdom, the king knows every one of His subjects personally. For, He has made us all. And despite our human failures, and rebellion, loves 'us', the humans, so much that He gives us all 'individual invitations'. This is not just for a brief visit, but also to stay forever in His kingdom, if we want to, and ask for it.

This king is willing to treat, each of us as 'His child' and offers to protect and provide for each. [The board and lodging is free!]

There is no tax levied in this kingdom. There is no sickness or death and therefore no health expenses. There are no tears, worries, anxieties, anger, fear, depressions, and no physical, mental, or moral sickness. We have purpose, prosperity, security and eternal joy when we live in God's kingdom.

The roads are paved with gold, the walls and gates are made of precious jewels. [There was a great gold rush to California and Alaska. But the gold had petered-out and so did the people who went after the gold.] If people don't rush to get into such a kingdom, they lose the opportunity to obtain citizenship in a kingdom that offers security, eternal life, health, wealth, peace and love.

Even terrorists are given an opportunity to repent and apply for immigration and naturalization. Each individual applicant is selected and given an orientation personally by Jesus Christ, and the Holy Spirit. The applicant's fee is to have trust and faith in the Lord Jesus Christ [INS], who will accept all [however unfit or wretched] who really want to become God's subjects. During this process, God adopts us as His Children. For, we became separated from God when sin entered into us. [Such a separation was, and is, to be "Dead" to God eternally.]

In order to be reunited with God, we need to be born-again in our spirit, which had died in sin. Those who accept the Royal invitation from God, sent through the Lord Jesus Christ repent of their sins and want to be in God's family. Those who are willing to become God's subjects will then be given the basic education on earth to learn the heavenly language- love and prayer, to keep in touch with the king. This process is one of progressive adaptation to enable us to live in the pristine pure, holy and, loving atmosphere of the Father's kingdom.

Transportation and reception into this kingdom are free. Material possessions will be left behind, along with those who have rejected the free invitation to this kingdom. Unlike worldly kingdoms, God's kingdom has no end and is absolutely invincible.

Chapter 4

ACCEPTING THE RESPONSIBILITIES OF CITIZENSHIP

INS related questionnaire, with answers and explanations.

1]. Question: - Can all humanity call God as "Father"?

Answer: - Some contend that the Lord's Prayer is applicable only to those predestined. What they need to recognize is that it is not for us humans to select. The discernment of who is to be elected or selected is in the Father's hand. The invitation is for all, but God in His foresight knows who will accept His invitation, and who will turn it down,

Application: - *John 10:16 (NLT) I have other sheep, too, that are not in this sheepfold. I must bring them also, and they will listen to my voice; and there will be one flock with one shepherd.*

Psalm 86:5 (NLT) O Lord, you are so good, so ready to forgive, so full of unfailing love for all who ask your aid.

2]. Question:-What about the educated scholars who say that there is no God, or Creator, and that we have evolved from various non-livings to living organisms?

Answer: - God's offer is rejected by those who are ignorant and unaware of their [parentage] Father; or, those who have turned away from Him [in anger]. How true it is that there are no fools greater than those educated, but, who choose to be foolish.

The present state of mind of humanity is repeatedly being manipulated and misled by people who are proud, and arrogant. They have self-destructive ideas. They struggle to prove to themselves and to others that there is no God. This is because they do not want to be accountable; or, because of their personal opinions, and failure of seeking for real truth. They try to brainwash, or, force the rest of the world to believe the ridiculous ideas that they possess. School and college text books, and T.V. shows are commonly used as brain washing tools.

Each pseudo-scientist tries to outdo the previous one by coining terrestrial and celestial 'lies' to mix with the real currency.[Lies are usually smuggled, lying on the back of slim or partial truths] When these so called scholars do not know who their own great- great- grand parents were, they are absurdly sure of what happened, not only many millions, even billions of years ago! They even desperately want to believe that they evolved from primates (monkeys), dogs and pigs, and even worse, that they have really evolved from slime and worms. People with such ideas and beliefs; do not want to be accountable to anyone, including their maker. If they acknowledge God as the Creator, then, they have to obey His laws, find-out the purpose for their existence and make an honest effort to fulfill it. They have to account for their various thoughts, words and actions to this Creator. This, they do not want. They do not want to believe that they are in need of any Divine help or Redemption from sin and evil.

By accepting the theory of evolution, they can justify their predatory life style. Evolution implies and encourages that only the fittest should survive, and, that the rest are there to be preyed upon physically, morally, financially, or any otherwise. They therefore, rebelliously, reject God's invitation to call him as Father. Surprisingly, in spite of their insulting attitude, God in His mercy still keeps the invitation open, but only till their life-time on earth.

There are now many evolutional proponents who have rejected their past rebellion and come to call upon God as their Father.

There are some other wishful thinkers who believe that they have goodness and godliness built into them! They believe that there probably was a big 'bang' of the 'deity' who expanded, underwent fragmentation to make human beings. And that like an accordion, the universe and the deity will contract to come together, and fuse. This they want to believe should take a number of recycling and birth processes. Such people do not want to believe in the holiness, or, the justice of God. Morality for them is not a necessity but a relative term. They want to believe that they have no need of a loving, holy, and, just heavenly Father. They hope that multiple reincarnated lives will cancel-out their evils.

<u>Assurance</u>: - *Psalm 14:1 The fool hath said in his heart, There is no God. They are corrupt, they have done abominable works, there is none that doeth good.*

Psalm 53:1 Only fools say in their hearts, "There is no God." They are corrupt, and their actions are evil; no one does well!

3]. <u>Question</u>: - Who can call God as "Father"?

<u>Answer</u>: - Only those whose conscience responds to the loving Father's call, and who come to God with a broken and contrite heart.

4]. **Question**: - Why would you want to call God as "Father"?

Answer: - You, the reader will have to answer this question.

The women's liberation movement- 'feminists' are challenging the word 'Father God'. They want to change the name to 'mother goddess'! They are even trying to change the Bible!. There are many subtle and open worship of 'mother goddess' in both the so-called Christian and non-christen groups of people around the world. God the Creator is beyond the genders of male and female. As the Creator of the entire universe and all humanity, for His protection, and provision, He is called the Father. On earth, the mother's role is to nurse the offspring maturity, and have an influence on the behavior and life style of the offspring. God, on the other hand, gives the freedom of choice to humanity and does not smother them, or make robots of them to His mighty will. People, who have their heads into the flesh pot, cannot see what is in store for them above in God's Kingdom, where sex and flesh have no part. They cannot hold on to sex or their bodies, except for a brief earthly adult life time any way. If they have any sense, it is better for them to plan for their future in the Father's kingdom.

Assurance: - *Matthew 22:28-30 Therefore in the resurrection whose wife shall she be of the seven? for they all had her. [29] Jesus answered and said unto them, Ye do err, not knowing the scriptures, nor the power of God. [30]*

For in the resurrection they neither marry, nor are given in marriage, but are as the angels of God in heaven.

1 John 4:10 This is real love. It is not that we loved God, but that he loved us and sent his Son as a sacrifice to take away our sins.

5]. Question: - Do you want God's qualities to be in you?

Answer: - Though I am not worthy and am only a mud vessel, God can put His treasures [more precious than diamonds, rubies] such as Love, Joy, Peace, Long-suffering, Gentleness, Goodness, Faith, Meekness, and Temperance into this vessel of mine, the physical body.

Assurance: - *Matthew 21:22 And all things, whatsoever ye shall ask in prayer, believing, ye shall receive.*

James 4:3 Ye ask, and receive not, because ye ask amiss, that ye may consume it upon your lusts.

6]. Question: - Can we, mere mortals, resemble, or develop any resemblance to God the Father?

Answer: - In a good family, the children admire their father and would like to resemble and be like the father. When it comes to the [only perfect Father] most holy, loving, merciful and kind God, there should be no question. "God, the Father has assured us that when we really learn to love Him, we can be like Him and resemble Him."

Assurance: - *1 John 2:15 Stop loving this evil world and all that it offers you, for when you love the world, you show that you do not have the love of the Father in you.*

7]. Question: - How do I know that I love the Father?

Answer: - In answer I can only say this prayer. "Lord, I am unable: Please enable. I do realize that this is Your first commandment, obeying which will enable me to live to please You".

Assurance: - *John 21:16 Jesus repeated the question: "Simon son of John, do you love me?" "Yes, Lord," Peter said, "you know I love you." "Then take care of my sheep," Jesus said.*

8]. Question: - Do you obey your Father?

Answer: - Knowledge and wisdom will not be sufficient or effective in-order to function, till the understanding leads us to an absolute 'Obedience' to the all knowing Father's will. 'Love your neighbors' is God's second command to us

Assurance: - *John 15:17 I command you to love each other.*

9]. Question: - Do you consider yourself as the only elite and special one who deserves to be called a "child of God"?

Answer: - God has said that human hearts are desperately wicked and there is no one good, no, not one. Ask God to give you His evaluation.

Jeremiah 17:9 "The human heart is most deceitful and desperately wicked. Who really knows how bad it is?

Psalm 51:5 For I was born a sinner—yes, from the moment my mother conceived me.

10]. Question: - Who do you think are not the children of God and why?

Answer: - I do not know; only God knows. Saul who perse-
cuted Christians became Paul the apostle. The thief
on the cross became the first to taste the salvation
offered by the Lord Jesus, while He was still on the
Cross.

Assurance: - *Acts 9:15 But the Lord said, "Go and do what I
say. For Saul is my chosen instrument to take my message to the Gentiles and to kings, as well as to the
people of Israel.*

*Luke 23:40-43 But the other criminal protested, "Don't
you fear God even when you are dying? [41] We deserve
to die for our evil deeds, but this man hasn't done anything wrong." [42] Then he said, "Jesus, remember me
when you come into your Kingdom." [43] And Jesus
replied, "I assure you, today you will be with me in par-
adise."*

*Matthew 25:41-45 "Then the King will turn to those on
the left and say, 'Away with you, you cursed ones, into
the eternal fire prepared for the Devil and his demons!
[42] For I was hungry, and you didn't feed me. I was
thirsty, and you didn't give me anything to drink. [43] I
was a stranger, and you didn't invite me into your
home. I was naked, and you gave me no clothing. I was
sick and in prison, and you didn't visit me.' [44] "Then
they will reply, 'Lord, when did we ever see you hungry
or thirsty or a stranger or naked or sick or in prison,
and not help you?' [45] And he will answer, 'I assure
you, when you refused to help the least of these my
brothers and sisters; you were refusing to help me.'*

11]. **Question**: - Are you willing to be taught by your Father?

Answer: - My answer is yes. For, there is no better teacher.
Who is yours?

Assurance: - *Psalm 119:12 Blessed are you, O Lord; teach me your principles. Psalm 119:26 I told you my plans, and you answered. Now teach me your principles.*

Psalm 119:66 I believe in your commands; now teach me good judgment and knowledge.

12]. Question: - Are you willing to be disciplined by your Father?

Answer: - When my God [Jesus Christ] considered it necessary to be chastised for me, it is alright for me to be chastised by Him. For I know that whatever He does is out of His love for me and to make me a better person.

Assurance: - *Hebrews 12:6-9 For the Lord disciplines those he loves, and he punishes those he accepts as his children." As you endure this divine discipline, remember that God is treating you as his own children. Whoever heard of a child who was never disciplined? [8] If God doesn't discipline you as he does all of his children, it means that you are illegitimate and are not really his children after all. [9] Since we respect our earthly fathers who disciplined us, should we not all the more cheerfully submit to the discipline of our heavenly Father and live forever?*

Isaiah 53:5 But he was wounded for our transgressions, he was bruised for our iniquities: the chastisement of our peace was upon him; and with his stripes we are healed.

Deut. 8:5 So you should realize that just as a parent disciplines a child, the Lord your God disciplines you to help you.

13]. Question: - Why do you call yourself a child of God?

Answer: - The Father found me in sin's gutter, unable to get out on my own. Jesus Christ took me out, cleansed me, pardoned me at Calvary and gave me a glimmer of understanding of His great sacrifice for my sake. I still want to be considered only as His servant, but the Holy Spirit of God, put into my spirit and soul, keeps calling me and assuring me that I am God's child.

Assurance: - *Romans 8:33-34 Who dares accuse us whom God has chosen for his own? Will God? No! He is the one who has given us right standing with himself. [34] Who then will condemn us? Will Christ Jesus? No, for he is the one who died for us and was raised to life for us and is sitting at the place of highest honor next to God, pleading for us.*

Romans 8:38-39) And I am convinced that nothing can ever separate us from his love. Death can't, and life can't. The angels can't, and the demons can't. Our fears for today, our worries about tomorrow, and even the powers of hell can't keep God's love away. [39] Whether we are high above the sky or in the deepest ocean, nothing in all creation will ever be able to separate us from the love of God that is revealed in Christ Jesus our Lord.

14]. Question: - Do you want God to be your Father?

Answer: - It's up to you.

Assurance: - *Matthew 23:9 And don't address anyone here on earth as 'Father,' for only God in heaven is your spiritual Father.*

15]. Question: - What proof would you present to show others that you are a child of God?

Answer: - The assurance given by God. My priorities have changed. He found me in the gutter, not knowing a better way to live. He did not leave me where He found me, but took me out, cleansed me from my guilt, showed me the right way to live, and without forcing me, is willing to walk with me, pick me up when I fall or slip, calls me back when I wander, showing me what it is to love like God does.

Assurance: - *1 John 5:2 By this we know that we love the children of God, when we love God, and keep his commandments.*

16]. Question: - Will God encourage, permit, or tolerate sibling rivalry? Why are there so many divisions and dissentions?

Answer: - Though God made each one of us, he has also made us quite different from one another, making each one unique. We not only look a little different from one-another, but have different outlooks while looking at the same thing. This is called a different point of view.

This condition given to us for our benefit should not make us expect others to look upon things only as we do. When we have diverse opinions on things we see and handle, how much more will we have upon God, whom we can't see with our mortal eyes. That is why the Bible, the word of God, is given to us, to help us focus and learns more about our Creator. Like the spokes in a wheel which converge and face each other when at the hub, Christ is our hub. We will be close and be focused at the hub, but then, each will diverge toward the rim of the wheel. Where the rubber meets the road, the spokes are directed away from each other to evenly transmit the pressure on the rim. Each has a placement and function, provided Christ is the hub, and love for God and God's love for others rule our lives.

Assurance: - *1 Cor. 1:10 Now, dear brothers and sisters, I appeal to you by the authority of the Lord Jesus Christ to stop arguing among yourselves. Let there be real harmony so there won't be divisions in the church. I plead with you to be of one mind, united in thought and purpose*

Romans 16:17 And now I make one more appeal, my dear brothers and sisters. Watch out for people who cause divisions and upset people's faith by teaching things that are contrary to what you have been taught. Stay away from them.

17]. Question: - Can all the Christians in the churches use this prayer?

Answer: - Yes. There are no church denominations in heaven. The word of God says that only the ones, who repent, seek God and receive Jesus into their lives can call God as Father

Assurance: - *John 1:12-13 But to all who believed him and accepted him, he gave the right to become children of God. [13] They are reborn! This is not a physical birth resulting from human passion or plan—this rebirth comes from God*

18]. Question: - Are you qualified to use this prayer?

Answer: - Only you can answer this question.

Assurance: - *1 John 3:10 In this the children of God are manifest, and the children of the devil: whosoever doeth not righteousness is not of God, neither he that loveth not his brother.*

Try replacing "you" with "I" and "your" with "my" and ask yourself these questions.

Chapter 5

Secret of Success:
SUBMIT to the Father

a)   Request the gift of love, to be able to love our Creator and Father, in return of His love for us.

      Acknowledge the Father as our creator, not give in to the rebellious evolution lies of "God deniers", and "God defilers".

b)   Request the gift of love, to be able to love others who also have the privilege of calling the Creator as Abba Father.

c)   Request the gift of having the resemblance to our Father. (to resemble Him in His love, holiness, justice, so that it will be obvious to the beholder that we have the family likeness to show that we are indeed an image of God.)

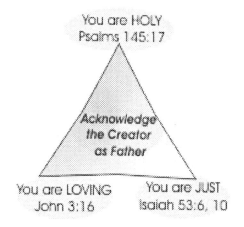

32

The Lord's Prayer

Establish KINSHIP

Our Father, who is in heaven:

OUR: - Note that the plural is used, indicating that God is not owned by any one. Neither I, nor any small groups have an *exclusive privilege* to call God as Father.

FATHER: - Acceptance by us, that we owe our existence to the Father. Accepting that God the Father is the ultimate Provider, Protector, Care giver, and the one who loves us.

HEAVEN: - Acceptance of the reality of Heaven indicates knowledge of the alternate place called Hell. Heaven is the Kingdom of God addressed in this prayer.

Hallowed be Thy name:

THE FATHER
Hallowed be Thy name

May your will be done

⊛ In our hearts and live's

⊛ In our homes

⊛ In our country

May your kingdom come

The word hallowed is a sacred word of absolute reverence, awe and worship. It is not comparable to the words 'hello' or 'hi' which are used as types of greetings.

If we are unfortunate enough to go to the court and face a very mortal human judge, we are expected to address him/her as "your honor," irrespective of whether they are honorable or not; the failing for which we can be fined or imprisoned for contempt of the court.

When we communicate with God, we must realize that we are not just saying "hi" to a man upstairs, [as some quip].

We are given an audience and given an instant admission to talk to the one who created the sun, moon, stars, galaxies, and the entire universe. He is the one who made each one of us and knows us even before our conception. We need to address such a God with reverence, gratitude, and love. The prayer tells us more about it.

Many leaders of the state or the church put on themselves crown or cloaks, setting themselves far above the rest. But all human leaders are meant to be mere standard bearers. God's messenger has no merit except to convey or carry out God's wishes, and to make sure that God's name is glorified. Many mortal monarchs and royalties assumed divinity upon themselves, but they are no more. When the Divine is willing to become your and my King, we need to revere, honor and hallow His Holiness, justice, mercy and love. A son, who commits atrocious crimes and is caught, brings disgrace upon the family which is represented by the father. Many criminals own up to the basic fact that they came from broken homes, or, from homes without a good father. They had no father who provided, or cared, or spent time with them. The modern trend is not to accept responsibility but blame someone else for things going wrong, including blaming God Himself.

God the Father is Holy, Just, Merciful, and Loving. He is Almighty, All-knowing, was Present in the past, is present now, and will be present in the future, crossing the barrier of time and space. There is no weakness or injustice in Him. We are not able to understand the reason for the extent of His love for us, His rebellious creation. Even to the extent of His Grace, [meaning mercy,] toward the unmerited when He took our penalty upon Himself!

But it does not mean that He will turn a blind eye to our mounting sin.

Such a Father, God the Creator of all, needs to be held in high veneration, love, awe, and with humility by us. The duty is upon us not to disgrace such a Father.

The Old Testament scholars would not even dare utter the "name' of JEHOVA [or JAHWEH,] the name of the Father.

God's holiness and justice will have to be justified by His honest judgment of us, the human being. He is only delaying the Day of Judgment toward us, giving us a chance to get right.

Thy kingdom come:

Recognize KINGSHIP

KING or Monarch had absolute power over every one of His subjects, their lives and their property.

Every thought, desire, motive, word and every action should be subject to God and be under His rule. God should rule over us, completely. All glory, honor, and service are given to God, and we become His obedient, rejoicing, grateful subjects. To be a citizen of a great country of a great ruler has immense privileges. The king is bound to protect His subjects, and see to His subject's comfort, and care [health- benefits, retirement benefits, justice etc.] Many from different nations come to prosperous countries to become citizens, in-order to partake the benefits. The most prosperous country in the world is nothing compared to the Creator's Heavenly kingdom in which we are citizens.

Thy will be done on earth as it is in heaven:

Responsibility of CITIZENSHIP.

In countries, under monarchy, or a dictator, the leader has the final and absolute say. This action the leader believes will unify the nation and strengthen and stabilize it. Any one who is a dissenter is killed, or imprisoned or expelled as a threat to the national security. The king theoretically owns the kingdom, each and every subject. But in the, Democratic, Republic and Social systems, there are many 'dissensions', many traitors and many saboteurs because of individual opinions and selfishness. They further tend to weaken the leadership through the grapevine system or more boldly through the rebel media. When there can be as many differences promoted as there are people in a nation, it will weaken and destroy the nation.

But in the heavenly kingdom, though God is the absolute owner and ruler, there is no weakness. Each subject will love the other more than the 'self'. For, the heavenly kingdom inhabitants are aware that God, the Father loves them more. For, the heavenly kingdom inhabitants are well aware that God, the Father loves them most, putting Himself "on the line" for the least of His subject. As a loving Father should, this He has done. If the love for the Father is in His subjects, they too would want to know what God's will is and obey it, to please God. Heaven is more a home than a kingdom as we have seen on earth. We will be secure in the knowledge that God's love is so great that He has the best for us. Obedience is possible, only if Christ is Lord of one's life, and the Holy Spirit is the resident and president of one's will. It is only then that the person can come under the Father's will and rule. My desire and prayer is, "Just as God's will is carried out without questioning and with authority in heaven, so also let it be in my body, mind, soul and spirit, with an absolute obedience."

Chapter 6

ACCEPTING THE LORDSHIP OF THE SON OF GOD

SON
ADMIT

The Secret of Success, and its start,
Is to admit the Son into your heart.

Give us this day our daily bread.

Receiving the Son's LORDSHIP

TODAY: - **Each day, we eat to survive that day. We cannot eat for tomorrow, today. What we ate yesterday is not enough for today. We eat two to three times a day, and still would like to snack to keep us going for usually a few years, typically less than 80 years.**

To help us to live and last many thousands of centuries, for eternity we need to have proper nourishment, which is prayer.

Immature infants cry whether hungry or not. Parents feed the infant periodically, till the time the child matures to let them know whether it is hungry or not. If the infant is unable to cry for food, it still needs to be fed in order to live and grow. When mature enough to understand hunger he/she will seek food. If any grown up person goes to a new or different land where the language is strange, he or she will find it hard to obtain food or the raw material to prepare good food till he/she learns to ask for what is needed. One has to learn the local 'language' to survive. This is called prayer.

If some miscreant labels the raw material wrongly to have fun, or to spread terror, we become helpless. For we may get inedible material or even poisons mixed with the grocery or contaminated meat. The devil is well known to change the labels on many things. Cyanide had been put into pain-medications and food. So what do we do? Prayer and Hope are the only answer.

We need to admit that we are hungry and need food. We need to seek, and ask for food. We need to ask for the right food. We can't eat whatever looks good. Poison berries and poison mushroom may look good, but, if eaten, will make us very sick, and cause our painful death. We need food not only to satisfy our hunger, but also to nourish us and bring health, and life to us. Similarly we need Spiritual food that is [healthy] and is able to nourish and give us eternal life.

Jesus has offered to become our life giving food and life-giving water, to sustain us on earth as well as through eternity. On earth we have to pay dearly for food. God has given Jesus the Bread from heaven freely to us. As prophesied, Jesus was born in Bethlehem, alternatively named as the 'house of bread'.

He is our Manna from heaven: -

Exodus 16:4-5. Then the Lord said to Moses, "Look, I'm going to rain down food from heaven for you. The people can go out each day and pick up as much food as they need for that day. I will test them in this to see whether they will follow my instructions. Tell them to pick up twice as much as usual on the sixth day of each week."

Exodus 16:20-21 But, of course, some of them didn't listen and kept some of it until morning. By then it was full of maggots and had a terrible smell. And Moses was very angry with them. [21] The people gathered the food morning by morning, each family according to its need. And as the sun became hot, the food they had not picked up melted and disappeared.

Prayer, like Manna is needed for each day and sought for, every day. No one can pray on a day and think that it would cover for the coming few days!. Some go to church on Sunday morning and think that it will carry them till next Sunday morning.

Relying on prayer, for once a week

Will leave you, spiritually very weak

He is our daily Bread: -

John 6:32-33 Jesus said, "I assure you, Moses didn't give them bread from heaven. My Father did. And now he offers you the true bread from heaven. [33] The true bread of God is the one who comes down from heaven and gives life to the world."

He is the Bread, broken for us. He gave His very Blood to us as transfusion to save our lives and souls*: -*

> *1 Cor. 11:23-24 For this is what the Lord himself said, and I pass it on to you just as I received it. On the night when he was betrayed, the Lord Jesus took a loaf of bread, [24] and when he had given thanks, he broke it and said, "This is my body, which is given for you. Do this in remembrance of me."*

Jesus offers to meet all our hunger and thirst.

> *Matthew 5:6 Blessed are they which do hunger and thirst after righteousness: for they shall be filled.*

> *John 6:35 Jesus replied, "I am the bread of life. No one who comes to me will ever be hungry again. Those who believe in me will never thirst.*

The wonder and greatness of His offer is effective not only for a short duration like the best of worldly meal [till the hunger and thirst hits us again] after a few hours, but lasts through our entire physical life and operates throughout eternity.

John 4:13-14 Jesus replied, "People soon become thirsty again after drinking this water. [14] <u>But the water I give them takes away thirst altogether. It becomes a perpetual spring within them, giving them eternal life</u>. "John 4:32-34) "No," he said, "I have food you don't know about." [33] "Who brought it to him?" the disciples asked each other. [34] Then Jesus explained: "My nourishment comes from doing the will of God, who sent me, and from finishing his work.

Forgive us our trespasses

God came down to earth as Jesus, to seek us and to show us how we can live a life without sinning, even on earth. He also took upon Himself the just punishment due to us for our sins. This was because there was no other way for us to be forgiven by a God who is so absolutely holy and just. Justice demands retribution, punishment and restitution whether it is legal as on earth, or regal, as in heaven. Jesus took upon Himself, the sin of humanity especially during His prayer in Gethsemane. He knew that He had to be separated from the Holy Father from then on until His death and burial. But, then, He broke the power of sin upon humanity. He broke the power of Satan and death as He rose up, alive, three days later. He stayed on earth for forty days before ascending up to heaven. He was seen by hundreds of people after His resurrection, some of whom have documented the fact. He is the one who has the right and power to forgive any and all who call upon Him, repent of their sins, and believe on Him. They freely receive their pardon and salvation by receiving Jesus into their lives.

Hebrews 9:22 In fact, we can say that according to the law of Moses, nearly everything was purified by sprinkling with blood. <u>Without the shedding of blood, there is no forgiveness of sins</u>.

Animal sacrifices or mere sinful mortals cannot cleanse our sins. So God, out of His love for us, [which is totally unmerited] offered to be the penalty payer and sacrifice for us.

> *1 Cor. 5:7 Purge out therefore the old leaven that ye may be a new lump, as ye are unleavened. For even Christ our Passover is sacrificed for us:*

> *Romans 8:1-4 So now there is no condemnation for those who belong to Christ Jesus. [2] For the power of the life-giving Spirit has freed you through Christ Jesus from the power of sin that leads to death. [3] The law of Moses could not save us, because of our sinful nature. But God put into effect a different plan to save us. He sent his own Son in a human body like ours, except that ours are sinful. God destroyed sin's control over us by giving his Son as a sacrifice for our sins. [4] He did this so that the requirement of the law would be fully accomplished for us who no longer follow our sinful nature but instead follow the Spirit.*

Sin brings upon us an eternal curse. Only an eternal God can deliver us. Our own sincere and valiant-efforts, or self-penance however deep and well meant cannot deliver us. God had to take the curse upon Himself:-

> *Psalm 86:5 O Lord, you are so good, so ready to forgive, so full of unfailing love for all who ask your aid.*

> *Galatians 3:13 But Christ has rescued us from the curse pronounced by the law. When he was hung on the cross, he took upon himself the curse for our wrongdoing. For it is written in the Scriptures, "Cursed is everyone who is hung on a tree."*

Jesus spoke about this fact to His disciples and other listeners.

Matthew 20:28 For even I, the Son of Man, came here not to be served but to serve others, and to give my life as a ransom for many."

It should be noted that Jesus is the one and only God who came to save not only so-called god fearing good people, but also desperate sinners without any hope of heaven. If you acknowledge that you are a sinner, your only hope is in Jesus and His offer to be your substitute and salvation. Sinful people are guilty of sins of commission against God and mankind. But the so-called good people are guilty of the sin of omission by not receiving Jesus as Savior in their lives.

> *Romans 5:10 For since we were restored to friendship with God by the death of his Son while we were still his enemies, we will certainly be delivered from eternal punishment by his life.*

> *1 Peter 1:18-19 For you know that God paid a ransom to save you from the empty life you inherited from your ancestors. And the ransom he paid was not mere gold or silver. [19] He paid for you with the precious lifeblood of Christ, the sinless, spotless Lamb of God.*

God the Father wants you and me to trust Him, repent and accept the offer of free pardon and eternal salvation, effected through Jesus Christ.

Sadly we have programmed ourselves to be suspicious of any one offering us 'something' free. But this offer is from God who created us .We will make ourselves into 'nothing' if we reject God's loving offer made through Lord Jesus.

> *Romans 3:25-26 For God sent Jesus to take the punishment for our sins and to satisfy God's anger against us. <u>We are made right with God when we believe that Jesus shed his blood, sacrificing his life for us</u>. God was being*

44

entirely fair and just when he did not punish those who sinned in former times. [26] And he is entirely fair and just in this present time when he declares sinners to be right in his sight because they believe in Jesus.

2 Cor. 5:18-19 All this newness of life is from God, who brought us back to himself through what Christ did. And God has given us the task of reconciling people to him. [19] <u>For God was in Christ, reconciling the world to himself, no longer counting people's sins against them</u>. This is the wonderful message he has given us to tell others.

2 Cor. 5:21 <u>For God made Christ, who never sinned, to be the offering for our sin, so that we could be made right with God through Christ.</u>

1 John 2:2 He is the sacrifice for our sins<u>. He takes away not only our sins but also the sins of all the world.</u>

1 John 4:10 This is real love. It is not that we loved God, but that he loved us and sent his Son as a sacrifice to take away our sins.

When God says that He will forgive, it is absolutely, and not partially. There will be no records kept, no grudges, or black-marks held against any one forgiven.

Isaiah 43:25 <u>"I—yes, I alone—am the one who blots out your sins for my own sake and will never think of them again.</u>

Matthew 26:28 <u>for this is my blood, which seals the covenant between God and his people. It is poured out to forgive the sins of many.</u>

God makes a blood covenant with us, using, not our blood, but His own.

Isaiah 55:7 Let the wicked forsake his way, and the unrighteous man his thoughts: and let him return unto the Lord, and he will have mercy upon him; and to our God, for he will abundantly pardon.

Jeremiah 31:34 And they shall teach no more every man his neighbor, and every man his brother, saying, Know the Lord: for they shall all know me, from the least of them unto the greatest of them, saith the Lord; for I will forgive their iniquity, and I will remember their sin no more.

God will not only forgive us, but will also heal us of sin. This way, we will have a healthy start in our 'new' life.

James 5:15-16 And their prayer offered in faith will heal the sick, and the Lord will make them well. And anyone who has committed sins will be forgiven. [16] Confess your sins to each other and pray for each other so that you may be healed. The earnest prayer of a righteous person has great power and wonderful results.

Col. 1:14 God has purchased our freedom with his blood and has forgiven all our sins.

WE need to repent of our sins that were responsible for putting the Lord Jesus on the Cross. As the penalty of our sins was upon Him, we need to confess them humbly, not trying to hide, or, give excuses for any. We need to make restitutions and seek apology from people in matters convicted by the Spirit of God. This we can do only if we believe on God and His offer. This "Faith" on the word of God is acceptable to God the Father to make you a citizen of heaven. The Holy Spirit will come into your life, along with Jesus, to secure and assure you of eternal salvation.

Acts 2:38 Peter replied, "Each of you must turn from your sins and turn to God, and be baptized in the name of Jesus Christ for the forgiveness of your sins. Then you will receive the gift of the Holy Spirit.

Mere repentance or sorrow for sins, without faith in God's loving offer will bring into a person a total loss of hope and a deep 'self-condemnation'. Self-Condemnation is brought upon people by Satan to prevent them from putting their trust in God. When hope is lost, many commit suicide like Judas, the betrayer of Jesus did. The truth is, there is no sin that God will not forgive, and, no sinner who God cannot save. There is no way for hope to be lost with God.

> *Matthew 27:3-4 When Judas, who had betrayed him, realized that Jesus had been condemned to die, he was filled with remorse. So he took the thirty pieces of silver back to the leading priests and other leaders. [4] "I have sinned," he declared, "for I have betrayed an innocent man." "What do we care?" they retorted. "That's your problem."*

> *Acts 1:18 Judas bought a field with the money he received for his treachery, and falling there, he burst open, spilling out his intestines.*

Making restitution is not only good, but also necessary for those who have received forgiveness of their sins, so that others can also benefit. One of the good ways to start a new life is to make restitution, for errors of commission and omission. This will miraculously open the way to share the good news with others. If you keep silent, it makes you selfish, weak and does not make you walk in God's way. In fact, if you keep silent, it fosters disobedience in you. For Jesus wants us to share the good news with others.

> *Luke 1:77 You will tell his people how to find salvation through forgiveness of their sins.*

> *Luke 24:47) With my authority, take this message of repentance to all the nations, beginning in Jerusalem: 'There is forgiveness of sins for all who turn to me.'*

Chapter 7

Restoring RELATIONSHIP With Our NEIGHBORS, Even The Ones WE Don't Like

As we forgive those who trespass against us

[Help-us to forgive]

Jesus came into this world to forgive sinners including you and me. No one else has done this in the history of all the religions of the world. Even when being tortured and crucified, Jesus forgave His tormentors and murderers. He came not only to forgive and save us, but also to make us loving 'like' Him. Only when we are able to love God, we will be glad to be with God, for eternity in heaven, God's home. Our training on godly love starts here on earth. We are asked to forgive those who offend or even persecute us on earth. This is possible only if Jesus has come into your heart and mine as our Savior, and the Holy Spirit becomes our indwelling companion and guide. If we are not able to forgive our enemies, and others who provoke us, we need to repent and get right with God.

> *Matthew 6:14 "If you forgive those who sin against you, your heavenly Father will forgive you.*

> *Matthew 18:21-22 Then Peter came to him and asked, "Lord, how often should I forgive someone who sins against me? Seven times?" [22] "No!" Jesus replied, "seventy times seven!*

> *Ephes. 4:32 Instead, be kind to each other, tender-hearted, forgiving one another, just as God through Christ has forgiven you.*

If we need and expect forgiveness of our sins, [so that we can call God as our Father, and hope to live eternally in heaven,] we need to forgive others just as God forgives us, with no strings attached. Moreover, <u>God's second command is for us to love others more than we love ourselves. That means we should hold no grudges or resentments. We need to give-up our rights.</u> We need to seek God's will and accept whatever He permits willingly and gladly. For, all things are known to God, and nothing can happen to us without His will and permission.

> *Mark 11:25-26 And when ye stand praying, forgive, if ye have ought against any: that your Father also which is in heaven may forgive you your trespasses. [26] But if ye do not forgive, neither will your Father which is in heaven forgive your trespasses.*

Chapter 8

SUBMITTING to the DISCIPLESHIP by the HOLY SPIRIT.

The Holy Spirit
PERMIT

Holy Spirit - The Secret of Success is to PERMIT the Holy Spirit to become not only a 'Resident' in our hearts, but also to be elected by you and me as the all powerful, beloved 'President' to influence our thoughts, lives, words and every action.

In your life, permit God's Spirit to become a resident,
Over your thoughts, words, and action rule as president.

THE HOLY SPIRIT
Keep us from temptations

Deliver us
from evil

Sanctify and
Preserve

- BE A BELOVED PERMANENT RESIDENT
- BE OUR ALL POWERFUL PRESIDENT
- CREATE AND CONTROL OUR THOUGHTS
  WORDS AND OUR ACTIONS

Lead us not into temptation.

God does not tempt anyone. We misuse the freedom of choice the Holy Spirit gives to us and get into sin. We need to surrender our rights and privileges to God. Abuse of the choice and freedom given to us leads us into temptation.

Willingness for DISCIPLESHIP under the Holy-Spirit

When you admit the Son, [Jesus Christ] into your heart, the Holy Spirit is also admitted in as a permanent resident. He is there to advise you and help you throughout your life. He does not force you to obey. He not only shows you how to live a holy and victorious life, but also enable you to succeed. The Lord Jesus promised to send the Holy Spirit to us, to abide with-in-us after His death and resurrection. So whenever a person receives Jesus as the Lord, the Holy Spirit baptizes that person and indwells that one, all through the life. But because He advises and not asserts, and gives us the freedom of choice even against His advice, we mortals tend to take undue advantage, and run to and into temptation. This prayer is to ask the Holy Spirit to accept our <u>voluntarily surrender of our long-rope of freedom and to give to us implicit obedience to His will</u>.

Every day and every step of our way, we need to pray, "Thank You for Your love that makes You give me the freedom, the misuse of which often grieves You. I am sorry I hear only the loud clamors around and within me that I mostly miss or ignore your still, gentle soft voice. I whole-heartedly surrender this freedom back to You as a small and insignificant offering. Let me be dead to my 'self' and let Christ live in and through me. Empower and enable me only to live to please and serve You. I thank You for putting up with me. I ask this request through Christ, for whose sake You indwell me'. Amen.

> *John 14:16 And I will ask the Father, and he will give you another Counselor, who will never leave you.*

> *John 16:13 Howbeit when he, the Spirit of truth, is come, he will guide you into all truth: for he shall not speak of himself; but whatsoever he shall hear, that shall he speak: and he will shew you things to come.*

> *James 1:13 And remember, no one who wants to do wrong should ever say, "God is tempting me." God is never tempted to do wrong and he never tempts anyone else either.*

When we receive the Lord Jesus as our personal Savior and Lord, we are born into God's kingdom, born of the Spirit. And the Holy –Spirit baptizes each one of us. The Holy Spirit gives us the spiritual inheritance of holy DNA, [Divine Nature Added] and, one or more characters of God, who now is our Father. We may consider them as gifts given to us by the Holy Spirit. These gifts may vary, but they need to be part of God' nature.

> *Romans 8:14 For all who are led by the Spirit of God are children of God.*

> *1 Cor. 12:7-11 A spiritual gift is given to each of us as a means of helping the entire church. [8] To one person the Spirit gives the ability to give wise advice; to another he gives the gift of special knowledge. [9] The Spirit gives special faith to another, and to someone else he gives the power to heal the sick. [10] He gives one person the power to perform miracles, and to another the ability to prophesy. He gives someone else the ability to know whether it is really the Spirit of God or*

another spirit that is speaking. Still another person is given the ability to speak in unknown languages, and another is given the ability to interpret what is being said. [11] It is the one and only Holy Spirit who distributes these gifts. He alone decides which gift each person should have.

Different gifts are given to different individuals within a corporate body to make the body viable and capable of functioning well. God has not made us independent but inter-dependant. Even the muscles in the body have diametrically opposite functions to keep them healthy and functional. [e.g.:- flexors against extensors, adductors against abductors in the body].

1 Cor. 12:21 The eye can never say to the hand, "I don't need you." The head can't say to the feet, "I don't need you."

1 Cor. 12:7 A spiritual gift is given to each of us as a means of helping the entire church.

The Holy Spirit teaches and gives us guidance.

John 16:12-15 "Oh, there is so much more I want to tell you, but you can't bear it now. [13] When the Spirit of truth comes; he will guide you into all truth. He will not be presenting his own ideas; he will be telling you what he has heard. He will tell you about the future. [14] He will bring me glory by revealing to you whatever he receives from me. [15] All that the Father has is mine; this is what I mean when I say that the Spirit will reveal to you whatever he receives from me.

There will be times in our earthly life when we get shaken because of various trials and temptations. We may wonder if we really are born into God's kingdom. These fears and doubts are flung at us by Satan to make us ineffective cowards. At such times, we need to listen more closely to the indwelling Holy Spirit, for He gives us assurance of our eternal salvation, and strengthens our Faith in God our Father.

> *Romans 8:16 For his Holy Spirit speaks to us deep in our hearts and tells us that we are God's children.*

The Holy Spirit sets up a communication link between us and our Father in heaven. He keeps the line clean and clear. He teaches us how to pray, and joins with us to help us learn the phonics of the heavenly language, which is love. This love is not only Love for God, also God's Love for other human beings, flowing through us. It is only then our prayers will not be selfish, but become a loving concern for others, just like what the Lord Jesus, the Holy Spirit and the Father have.

> *Romans 8:26 And the Holy Spirit helps us in our distress. For we don't even know what we should pray for, nor how we should pray. But the Holy Spirit prays for us with groanings that cannot be expressed in words.*

> *Ephes. 6:18-19 Pray at all times and on every occasion in the power of the Holy Spirit. Stay alert and be persistent in your prayers for all Christians everywhere.*

Chapter 9

Enlist into God's Royal Marines- 'WARSHIP' to Battle against evil

There are two armies in this world. There are no civilians or neutrals. One is the holy army of God, and the other is the evil one of Satan's. Any one who does not get into God's army is automatically drafted into Satan's army. Like the aerial reconnaissance planes, The Holy –Spirit reveals to us the enemy positions, strength, and movements, and how to avoid or overcome them.

He also keeps us constantly aware of our position and relationship to God [supply line], and our position in the battlefield so that we can advance or avoid and follow His aerial directions. If we don't take the guidance from the Holy Spirit, and fail to, or, refuse His guidance, we will suffer heavy casualty. [We may hurt, and shoot our own team members, alas many churches do this] It is absolutely necessary for us to <u>Trust and Obey</u> His orders to become victors. He empowers us, and enables us. Satan seduces us through our flesh, which, having been made of earthly dirt, is weak, dirty, and easily susceptible to dirty sin. The spirit within us, having been born of heavenly Spirit is meant for eternity. Our temporal flesh does not easily accept the Spirit's control and rebels continuously. The mind, which always wants to have the final say and choice, is reluctant to allow the Holy Spirit to take the ultimate control. It is however necessary for the mind and the flesh to submit and yield into the heavenly wisdom of the Holy Spirit.

> *Galatians 5:16-23 So <u>I advise you to live according to your new life in the Holy Spirit. Then you won't be doing what your sinful nature craves.</u> [17] The old sinful nature loves to do evil, which is just opposite from*

what the Holy Spirit wants. And the Spirit gives us desires that are opposite from what the sinful nature desires. These two forces are constantly fighting each other, and your choices are never free from this conflict. [18] But when you are directed by the Holy Spirit, you are no longer subject to the law. [19] When you follow the desires of your sinful nature, your lives will produce these evil results: sexual immorality, impure thoughts, eagerness for lustful pleasure, [20] idolatry, participation in demonic activities, hostility, quarreling, jealousy, outbursts of anger, selfish ambition, divisions, the feeling that everyone is wrong except those in your own little group, [21] envy, drunkenness, wild parties, and other kinds of sin. Let me tell you again, as I have before, that anyone living that sort of life will not inherit the Kingdom of God. [22] But when the Holy Spirit controls our lives, he will produce this kind of fruit in us: love, joy, peace, patience, kindness, goodness, faithfulness, [23] gentleness, and self-control. Here there is no conflict with the law.

But deliver us from evil.

When we yield to the Holy Spirit to operate in our lives without any opposition, He will start and take us through a process of sanctification and consecration. He does this from within-out [starting from our inner most spirit and the conscience. Then He will work on our soul with its will. Then He will work upon our 'psycho-soma' with our desires, emotions, and thought-patterns. Eventually He will work on our physical body with its sensations, reactions, satiations, direction and control of our physiological and emotional urges practically turning us inside out]! During this process, He nurtures our spirit to grow in the image of God the Father, as God had planned. He takes us to the Cross where Christ fought and won the battle against evil. He enables us to find our relational position with the resurrected Jesus, so that we will have the victory in our daily lives to live like Jesus. For, then it will not be "we" but the triumphant Jesus living in and through "us".

We, learn from even the latest battle news that there is more fatal and crippling casualties during "Friendly-Firing' rather than from the enemy fire. We need grace and love to refrain from 'Infighting' with other believers located at different positions from us. We need to be controlled by the aerial instructions from the Coordinator of the spiritual battle. When we are not hidden or hiding from one another and the Master Planner, we will become like the transparent lamp glass, and He, the Light source, will be shining for others, to show them the Way, the Truth And His Life. The Truth [Light] will set anyone free, but only when it is believed and obeyed.

> *Romans 7:14-25 The law is good, then. The trouble is not with the law but with me, because I am sold into slavery, with sin as my master. [15] I don't understand myself at all, for I really want to do what is right, but I don't do it. Instead, I do the very thing I hate. [16] I know perfectly well that what I am doing is wrong, and my bad conscience shows that I agree that the law is good. [17] But I can't help myself, because it is sin*

inside me that makes me do these evil things. 18] I know I am rotten through and through so far as my old sinful nature is concerned. No matter which way I turn, I can't make myself do right. I want to, but I can't. [19] When I want to do good, I don't. And when I try not to do wrong, I do it anyway. [20] But if I am doing what I don't want to do, I am not really the one doing it; the sin within me is doing it.

[21] It seems to be a fact of life that when I want to do what is right, I inevitably do what is wrong. [22] I love God's law with all my heart. [23] But there is another law at work within me that is at war with my mind. This law wins the fight and makes me a slave to the sin that is still within me. [24] Oh, what a miserable person I am! Who will free me from this life that is dominated by sin? [25] Thank God! The answer is in Jesus Christ our Lord. So you see how it is: In my mind I really want to obey God's law, but because of my sinful nature I am a slave to sin.

2 Tim. 4:18 Yes, and the Lord will deliver me from every evil attack and will bring me safely to his heavenly Kingdom. To God be the glory forever and ever. Amen.

Romans 8:4 He did this so that the requirement of the law would be fully accomplished for us who no longer follow our sinful nature but instead follow the Spirit.

Galatians 5:16-18 So I advise you to live according to your new life in the Holy Spirit. Then you won't be doing what your sinful nature craves. [17] The old sinful nature loves to do evil, which is just opposite from what the Holy Spirit wants. And the Spirit gives us desires that are opposite from what the sinful nature desires. These two forces are constantly fighting each other, and your choices are never free from this conflict. [18] But when you are directed by the Holy Spirit, you are no longer subject to the law.

Galatians 5:25 If we are living now by the Holy Spirit, let us follow the Holy Spirit's leading in every part of our lives.

Romans 8:11-13 The Spirit of God, who raised Jesus from the dead, lives in you. And just as he raised Christ from the dead, he will give life to your mortal body by this same Spirit living within you.

Romans 8:16 For his Holy Spirit speaks to us deep in our hearts and tells us that we are God's children.

Romans 15:16 a special messenger from Christ Jesus to you Gentiles. I bring you the Good News and offer you up as a fragrant sacrifice to God so that you might be pure and pleasing to him by the Holy Spirit.

1 Cor. 6:11 There was a time when some of you were just like that, but now your sins have been washed away, and you have been set apart for God. You have been made right with God because of what the Lord Jesus Christ and the Spirit of our God have done for you.

2 Thes. 2:13 As for us, we always thank God for you, dear brothers and sisters loved by the Lord. We are thankful that God chose you to be among the first to experience salvation, a salvation that came through <u>the Spirit who makes you holy</u> and by your belief in the truth.

1 Peter 1:2 <u>God the Father chose you long ago, and the Spirit has made you holy. As a result, you have obeyed Jesus Christ and are cleansed by his blood.</u> May you have more and more of God's special favor and wonderful peace.

Chapter 10

Learning to WORSHIP the TRIUNE GOD

The role of Trinity in the Lord's Prayer

Begin to WORSHIP

For, Thine is the kingdom ------------The Father,

Ephes. 4:6 and <u>there is only one God and Father, who</u>
<u>is over us all and in us all and living through us all,</u>

Psalm 95:3-5 <u>For the Lord is a great God, the great</u>
<u>King above all gods, [4] He owns the depths of the</u>
<u>earth, and even the mightiest mountains are his, [5]</u>
<u>The sea belongs to him, for he made it. His hands</u>
<u>formed the dry land, too</u>.

And the Power ------------The Holy Spirit

Acts 1:8 <u>But when the Holy Spirit has come upon you,</u>
<u>you will receive power</u> and will tell people about me
everywhere—in Jerusalem, throughout Judea, in
Samaria, and to the ends of the earth."

Micah 3:8 But as for me, <u>I am filled with power and the</u>
<u>Spirit of the Lord</u>. I am filled with justice and might,
fearlessly pointing out Israel's sin and rebellion.

And the Glory ------------The Son - Jesus

1 Cor. 2:8 Which none of the princes of this world knew: for had they known it, they would not have <u>crucified the Lord of glory</u>.

2 Thes. 1:12 <u>That the name of our Lord Jesus Christ may be glorified in you,</u> and ye in him, according to the grace of our God and the Lord Jesus Christ.

John 12:23-28 Jesus replied, "<u>The time has come for the Son of Man to enter into his glory</u>. [24] The truth is a kernel of wheat must be planted in the soil. Unless it dies it will be alone—a single seed. But its death will produce many new kernels—a plentiful harvest of new lives. [25] Those who love their life in this world will lose it. Those who despise their life in this world will keep it for eternal life. [26] All those who want to be my disciples must come and follow me, because my servants must be where I am. And if they follow me, the Father will honor them. [27] Now my soul is deeply troubled. Should I pray, 'Father, save me from what lies ahead'? <u>But that is the very reason why I came! [28] Father, bring glory to your name</u>." Then a voice spoke from heaven, saying, "<u>I have already brought it glory, and I will do it again</u>."

Romans 6:13 Do not let any part of your body become a tool of wickedness, to be used for sinning. Instead, give yourselves completely to God since you have been given new life. <u>And use your whole body as a tool to do what is right for the glory of God.</u>

Romans 15:7 So <u>accept each other just as Christ has accepted you; then God will be glorified</u>.

2 Cor. 3:18 And all of us have had that veil removed so <u>that we can be mirrors that brightly reflect the glory of the Lord</u>. And as the <u>Spirit of the Lord works within us,</u>

we become more and more like him and reflect his glory even more.

2 Cor. 4:15 All of these things are for your benefit. And as God's grace brings more and more people to Christ, there will be great thanksgiving, and God will receive more and more glory.

2 Thes. 1:12 That the name of our Lord Jesus Christ may be glorified in you, and ye in him, according to the grace of our God and the Lord Jesus Christ.

Forever and ever, Amen